Out of Darkness:
Into the Light

Out of Darkness: Into the Light

A KJV STUDY OF II PETER 1:5-9

Patricia H. Nelson

WestBow
PRESS
A DIVISION OF THOMAS NELSON

WestBow Press books may be ordered through booksellers or by contacting:

WestBow Press
A Division of Thomas Nelson
1663 Liberty Drive
Bloomington, IN 47403
www.westbowpress.com
1-(866) 928-1240

ISBN: 978-1-4497-2457-3 (e)
ISBN: 978-1-4497-2458-0 (sc)

Library of Congress Control Number: 2011914928

Printed in the United States of America

WestBow Press rev. date: 09/15/2011

For my family:

My husband and best friend, Mark,
who has given me encouragement to follow through
with what God has burdened me to do.

My son, Ned, who, at sixteen, faced cancer and displayed
more courage than I could imagine and who knows
how to lift my spirits with a hug.

My daughter, Grace, who makes us laugh,
adds drama to our lives, and makes simple statements
that so sum up what God is trying to teach me.

My mom and dad, who brought us up in a God-fearing home
and faced adversity with faith. They always sought
to make the best of whatever came.

CONTENTS

Preface

I am not wise or good or righteous. I have tasted of the bread of life and can testify that He satisfies the hungry soul. Jesus is my salvation, my rock, my protector, my strength, and the light of my life. My efforts here on earth can bring momentary satisfaction: a clean house, a good meal cooked, and a job well done. Worldly entertainment can bring momentary delight. Yet when I long for lasting satisfaction in my soul, Jesus only is the answer. When I long for strength to make it through a day full of turmoil, Jesus only is the answer. When I long for true joy, Jesus only is the answer. When I long for contentment in difficult situations, Jesus only is the answer.

This study began as a longing to know Jesus better. What were notes about 2 Peter 1:5-9 twenty-three years ago became the basis for what you hold in your hands. I have carried a burden to testify about what He has done for me for quite a few years. Was I adequate to accept this responsibility? Absolutely not. Jesus has said He will use the foolish, the unlearned, and the weak to testify. My sincere prayer is that you see only Him in this study. Jesus's mercy, grace, and forgiveness have brought me thus far and will bring me face to face with Him.

I trusted Jesus as my Savior many years ago, and He gave me eternal life. Why are we so eager to lay claim to life after death but so hesitant to claim life while here on earth? He died and rose *not* only to give us a place with Him in heaven but to give us *abundant life* while here on earth. What is our duty? To daily submit, to believe, to trust Him with all our heart, and to lean not unto our own understanding. Taste and see that the Lord is good.

Chapter 1

INTRODUCTION: THE LIGHT

The mere fact that you have this study in your hands reveals that you have a desire to know more about the One who brought light to the world. If your motivation for being involved in a Bible study is that you desire to learn, you will be blessed (not by anything I have written but because of that desire). Take time to pray that God will speak to you through his Word.

Ephesians 3:12: "In whom we have boldness and access with confidence by the faith of him." How awesome that we can confidently ask Him to speak to us through His word. Please note that our boldness and confidence have absolutely nothing to do with us.

Read Proverbs 2:1-9. The level of our commitment to Him will be reflected in the amount of time and effort spent in searching the Scriptures for hidden treasure.

Before you commit to the study of God's Word, please consider Philippians 3:10. Note the four statements Paul made in this passage. If you are saved, then you know Jesus. Paul's words thereafter are clear and simple instructions for a submitted life. Note that they are simple, but not necessarily easy, steps we must take in order to live an abundant life in Christ. Do you desire to be brought to abundant life?

When you accepted Jesus as your Savior, His life was planted in you by the Holy Spirit. To grow spiritually, we must act upon the instruction given in the remainder of this verse.

1. *That I may know him and the power of his resurrection.* He is the resurrection and life. He makes us new creatures. Read Romans 6:4. We can joy in our salvation and His resurrected life in us, but do you long for more? There is more.

2. *The fellowship of his suffering.* We *must* accept that we will suffer. Do we long to know Him enough to suffer for His sake? Read Romans 8:17-18 and Psalm 34:19.

3. *Being made conformable unto his death.* When we were saved, we gave up our trying and trusted Him. Why then do we think that we can try and try and of our own efforts grow? Is that not self-righteousness instead of spiritual maturity?

Do you long to know Him enough to die? Read Galatians 2:20-21: "I am crucified with Christ: nevertheless I live; yet not I, but Christ liveth in me: and the life which I now live in the flesh I live by the faith of the Son of God, who loved me, and gave himself for me. I do not frustrate the grace of God; for if righteousness come by the law, then Christ is dead in vain."

What does it mean to die and yet live? We must let go of our reasoning and rights and submit to His control in our lives. Is there a part of us that feels that what He did on Calvary was not sufficient? Maybe we feel it was sufficient for our salvation but not for our lives. There must be no mistake. He did not die in vain. He is our faith, our growth, our joy, our peace, and our maturity. Only through our death to self and our willingness to suffer for Him can the *power* of His resurrection be released in our lives.

In this study, our focus will be 2 Peter 1:5-9:

"And beside this, giving all diligence, add to your faith virtue; and to virtue knowledge; and to knowledge temperance; and to temperance patience; and to patience godliness; and to godliness brotherly kindness; and to brotherly kindness charity. For if these things be in you, and abound, they make you that ye shall neither be barren nor unfruitful in the knowledge of our Lord Jesus Christ. But he that lacketh these things is blind, and cannot see afar off, and hath forgotten that he was purged from his old sins."

First, turn to 2 Peter 1 and read the four verses that precede the above Scripture. Who was Peter addressing in verse one?

_____

What promises are given in verses three and four?

_____

_____

_____

_____

How are we told in the beginning words of verse five to approach adding to our faith?

The principles named in 2 Peter 1:5-9 cannot be accomplished in our lives all at once. Learning about each principle should be ever continuing as long as we live. These principles are given to us in an order and thus should be studied in that order.

View the attributes given in this lesson as the very nature of Christ himself. Through salvation, we are granted access to these attributes by *His* power, not our own. See Him as the only source of light to your path. Jesus said in John 8:12, "I am the light of the world: he that followeth me shall not walk in darkness, but shall have the light of life." A lighthouse lights the path of ships in the darkness and in the storms so that they may safely travel. We live in a dark and stormy world. Jesus wants to light our way and warn us of danger. But we must be willing to look unto Him.

Spiritual growth can begin when we see the reality of John 15:5: "For without me ye can do nothing."

Philippians 4:13 says, "I can do all things through Christ which strengtheneth me."

These two verses present a beautiful comparison. Notice the words of John: "*without me* you can do nothing." And these are Paul's words: "I can do all things *through Christ*" (my emphasis).

Read 1 Corinthians 2:9. Salvation gives us access to the heart and mind of Christ. What a promise is made in verse nine.

The depth of our love for Him and our willingness to submit to Him are the keys to the treasure He alone possesses.

Read Proverbs 8:17-21. Summarize in your own words what these verses mean to you:

_____

_____

_____

_____

Satan would have us believe that the treasures of the world will satisfy our souls. Reread 2 Peter 1:8-9. What is the promise if we add to our faith virtue, knowledge, etc.?

_____

What is the warning in verse nine?

_____

_____

_____

_____

Consider Psalm 63. Note how our longing for Him is fulfilled if we truly seek Him. Is there a reason to come unto *The Light (Jesus)?* Is your heart satisfied? Do you long for the peace that passes understanding? What is the source of your strength? Let us all be encouraged to look unto Jesus as our light, to learn of Him, and to draw near Him so that the world will see His light in us.

Chapter 2

FAITH

What is faith?

Hebrews 11:1: "Now faith is the substance of things hoped for, the evidence of things not seen."

2 Corinthians 4:18: "While we look not at the things which are seen, but at the things which are not seen; for the things which are seen are temporal; but the things which are not seen are eternal."

So faith is something we can't see. Now read 2 Corinthians 5:7. How are we to walk?

_____

Faith is believing with all your heart and mind that God will do what He has promised. In order to be saved, you had to believe He would save you. Did you see Jesus with your eyes? No. But in your heart, you accepted Him as your Savior and trusted Him to save your soul.

Faith is the union of belief and trust. Faith in God should be a belief that is so strong it becomes a part of your nature. Our faith needs to be bigger than our feelings. What Paul refers to is a belief of the heart that is beyond an intellectual process since faith is the acceptance of the gospel as true. We did not see Jesus crucified. We did not see Him after He arose from the grave. But we can believe that it happened.

How do we walk by faith? To be faithful, one must be steady in devotion and unwavering in adherence to God's principles of life. Our faith is believing and accepting that the Lord is faithful to do as He has said. Trust is a practical and tranquil resting of the mind upon the integrity and promises of God.

Has He been faithful to you? That's the evidence! Take a few moments to think about ways He has been faithful to you. Thank Him for His faithfulness.

Our spiritual vision can be obscured because our minds cannot clearly discern or see since there is a lack of light. Psalm 27:1: "The Lord is my light and my salvation . . . ." The closer you are to the light, the more clearly you can see.

Proverbs 15:3 says, "The eyes of the Lord are in every place, beholding the evil and the good." Human reasoning and logic leave out God. So many times, we follow the secular or humanistic approach of believing only the things that we understand. Isaiah 55:8-9: "For my thoughts are not your thoughts, neither are your ways my ways, saith the Lord. For as the heavens are higher than the earth, so are my ways higher than your ways, and my thoughts than your thoughts."

Trusting our human reasoning and understanding is the fallacy that brings us to the general condition of the world today, as stated in Isaiah 5:20: "Woe unto them that call evil good, and good evil; that put darkness for light, and light for darkness; that put bitter for sweet, and sweet for bitter!"

Is there something God wants us to see? Yes! Read Proverbs 29:18: "Where there is no vision the people perish . . . ." What is that vision?

1) Seeing God for who he is! Through his Word, we can be touched by his love, his compassion, his mercy, and his care for every aspect of our lives. Look for the evidence of God at work in your own life.
2) Seeing ourselves as we are—we must be humbled at His feet.
3) Seeing His provision for our every need.

What about God can we begin to understand? His power, his greatness, and the qualities of His heart need to be magnified in our minds and hearts.

Read Exodus 34:1-7. What did the Lord call upon Moses to do?

_____

What qualities were named about the Lord in verses six and seven?

_____

_____

_____

_____

Read Isaiah 6:1-8. How did the prophet Isaiah see the Lord? (verse one)

_____

How did Isaiah see himself? (verse five)

_____

When he confessed his sins, was he forgiven? (verses six and seven)

_____

Now read verse eight again. Isaiah saw the Lord high and lifted up. He saw himself as a sinner. He confessed, his sins were purged, and then he was called to do a work. Only when we see Him as He is, ourselves as we are, and seek forgiveness can His purpose for us be fulfilled. When we see Him as He is and see ourselves as we are, we will no longer be pointing a finger at anyone else.

The greatness of God and His power is a subject that is far beyond me. It is my prayer that, through examination of the Scriptures, we can begin to see Him more clearly. As the Scripture we have read thus far clearly reflects, to see Him more clearly we first have to see ourselves as nothing.

We started this chapter with Hebrews 11:1. Look at Hebrews 11:6: "For without faith, it is impossible to please him; for he that cometh to God must believe that he is, and that he is a rewarder of them that diligently seek him."

Chapter 3

Faith: The Author and Finisher

In this chapter of study, let us examine Hebrews 11 and part of Hebrews 12. Read all of Hebrews 11 (commonly referred to as the "faith" chapter). The heroes of faith referred to in this chapter were not perfect people. They were sinners saved by grace, just like you and I. However they shared a common trait—a pursuit of faith in God and obedience to act with faith when called upon.

Who makes up the cloud of witnesses referred to in chapter twelve? They are those who have gone before us, including the faithful mentioned in chapter eleven. Hebrews 12:1 tells us to "lay aside every weight, and the sin which doth so easily beset us, and let us run with patience the race that is set before us." In other words, prepare yourself to run the race. Just as a runner preparing to run in a marathon, we must commit ourselves to the race. We must train ourselves (studying God's Word and praying) and resist the Devil when he tempts us to drop out of the race.

Hebrews 12:2 tells us that Jesus is not only the object of our faith but also the author. Our faith in Jesus began when we accepted Him as our Savior.

Now read Galatians 3:1-3. We received the Spirit by the hearing of faith (verse two). Are we made perfect by the flesh (verse three)? _____

Jesus also is the finisher of our faith (Hebrews 12:2). We must look to Him, not depending at all in our self-righteousness to complete His work in us.

1) We have a race to run. Our race is marked out clearly before us (Matthew 5:14-16). Read this Scripture and note what Jesus is saying to us:

_____

_____

_____

_____

_____

2) There is no promise of the race being easy (Matthew 5:10-12). Summarize the lesson in this passage:

_____

_____

_____

_____

_____

3) Jesus is the example we look to. He endured the cross, despising the shame, suffered the pains of hell, and was the victor. Verse two of Hebrews 12 says, "and is set down at the right hand of the throne of God." He is there to make intercession with God for us.

Why did He do this for me? I deserved only hell. Jesus's love for mankind caused Him to endure the cross so that we could escape hell. Note the second phase of verse two: "for the joy that was set before him."

Paul saw the concept of faith as a dynamic one, an activity that manifests itself in love. In Galatians 5:5-6, it is said, "faith which worketh by love." What does this mean in your personal life? Are we a reflection of love?

Turn to James 2:17-18: "Even so faith, if it hath not works, is dead, being alone. Yea, a man may say, Thou hast faith, and I have works: shew me thy faith without thy works, and I will shew thee my faith by my works." What does this mean to you?

_____

_____

_____

_____

We must take an active role (participate) in being used of God. Allow the Holy Spirit to lead in the things He wants you to do and then do them.

We so often try to see the big picture and look for some grand plan or scheme God has for us. Often we want glory for our good deeds. When we have that mind-set, He most certainly is not being glorified. Our lives are made up of days, hours, and minutes. Trusting God with *every* aspect of our lives on a minute-by-minute basis and leaving the results to Him frees us. He has given so many precious promises we can claim if we are obedient.

We need to give up all our rights to make plans, utter words, or think thoughts outside His will. Faith that He has *all* things under His control is our peace.

Spiritual maturity is reflected in how well we handle adversity. Through my own experience, it is easier to trust Him when I am faced with a loved one having cancer than trusting Him with the small adversities we face. Is trusting Him so woven into the fabric of your life that you feel his presence constantly? An unwillingness to bend our own desires and thought processes clearly reflects who is in control in our lives. Do we ever consider that the light that turned to red just before you approached could be God's protecting hand? Do you ever think the washing machine that breaks, requiring you stay at home to wait for a repairman, could keep you off the road and spare your life?

Turn to Isaiah 12:3. Please write this verse and commit it to memory.

_____

_____

_____

_____

Salvation grants us access to a well of faith that will never run dry. Faith in Jesus will allow us to run with patience and joy the race set before us. *He* will finish our faith if we are only willing.

Chapter 4

FAITH: OUR PURPOSE

As we have just learned, we need to see ourselves as sinners saved by grace, and all our righteousness as filthy rags. Read Isaiah 64:4-6. Does this make you feel unworthy? _____ It should! He alone is worthy of praise.

But see this: When we accepted Christ as our Savior, He came to live within us! When we let Him rule in our lives, He is glorified (not us) and that pleases Him. Let's examine Scriptures that reveal His concern for us and His desires for our lives.

Read Romans 8:28. What is the promise?

_____

_____

What do we have to do to receive the promise?

_____

Read Jeremiah 29:11-13. What kind of thoughts does the Lord have for our lives?

_____

_____

What is required of us? (verse thirteen)

_____

1 Corinthians 6:20 says, "For ye are bought with a price: therefore glorify God in your body and in your spirit, which are God's." We were bought with the blood of Jesus Christ and we have a purpose.

2 Corinthians 5:20 says we are "ambassadors for Christ."

Now read Philippians 1:6. Is God doing a work in you?

_____

Are you resisting Him? _____

Read Galatians 6:3. Is there any reason for us to have pride in ourselves?_____

We have already read 1 Corinthians 2:9. Reread this Scripture. Does this mean more to you now?

Accept His goodness and faithfulness and rejoice that He lives within you.

We will now examine Scriptures that reflect His provision for our every need:

1) Psalms 3:3 – _____;
2) Psalms 27:1 – _____;
3) Psalms 31:3 – _____;

4) Psalms 61:3 – _____ ;
5) Psalms 63:7 – _____ ;
6) Isaiah 26:3 – _____ ;
7) 2 Corinthians 5:17 – _____ ;
8) 2 Thessalonians 3:3 – The Lord is _____ , who shall _____ you, and keep you from.

We have looked at Scriptures that reflect what Jesus is willing to be for us. He is everything we need! Did you notice that these are conditional promises? We must acknowledge what we are, love Him, seek Him, and have faith (believe) that He is who he says He is and will do what He has said He will do. Claim these promises for yourself!

Now look at Matthew 17:20. Take time to find out how large a mustard seed is.

If you have a willing heart to accept His plan for your life, God will supply everything you need. We know Jesus's death on the cross was God's perfect plan. Reflect on how horrible this was for Jesus. But His words when He met His people after He arose were, "O, joy." We *must* believe that His will for our lives will ultimately bring joy.

Read Philippians 4:19: "But my God shall supply all your need according to his riches in glory by Christ Jesus."

Lastly, let me say that even though we have looked at quite a number of Scriptures, we have just scratched the surface of what

God can do for us through our faith. I would be remiss without the following Scripture, which I will quote for you:

Proverbs 3:5-6: "Trust in the Lord with all thine heart; and lean not unto thine own understanding. In all thy ways acknowledge him, and he shall direct thy paths."

One day I mentioned to my husband that I truly wanted to enjoy every day the Lord gave me. He asked, "What keeps you from enjoying life completely?" I relayed that worries or concerns over my children and other things caused me to feel heavy burdened. He said to me, "That is your fear." And then he simply said, "You know I have a fear of heights. When we are in the mountains, as long as I am standing on solid ground and there is a guardrail in front of me, I can enjoy the view." This so quickly became a beautiful picture to me. If I am trusting Jesus completely, I *am* on solid ground and there *is* a guardrail! The above Scripture from Proverbs 3:5-6 came to mind. *Through Him, I can enjoy the view!*

Chapter 5

VIRTUE

The meaning of *virtue* is moral excellence. Does this mean we can become sinless?

Read 1 John 1:8. What is the warning here?

_____

_____

If we cannot become sinless, how can we live virtuous lives?

_____

Virtue is goodness that is victorious through trial, temptation, and conflict. Virtue encompasses honesty, integrity, and excellence of character. In plain English, virtue is the opposite of evil and wickedness.

When we know we have sin in our lives, we are to confess, seek God's forgiveness, and ask Him to help us not to commit the same sin again.

Read Psalms 34:14. How are we to approach being *good?*

_____

Many times we have to sever association with certain people if their influence leads us astray. Read Proverbs 22:24-25. What kind of people are we warned about?

_____

Read 1 Thessalonians 5:22. What is being taught in this Scripture?

_____

_____

We may be very aware of sin in our lives. In this case, we probably have very troubled hearts because we feel convicted. We must confess, ask forgiveness, and turn away from this pattern of behavior.

When we repent, we are forgiven and made as clean as the moment we were saved. However, our sins have consequences. Read Galatians 6:7-9. What are we told about our sin in this Scripture?

_____

_____

Read Ephesians 4:25-32. List at least six virtuous qualities named in this passage:

1) _____ ;
2) _____ ;
3) _____ ;
4) _____ ;
5) _____ ;
6) _____ .

I once heard that taking the path of sin can be likened to the Israelites going to Egypt—bondage. When we are tempted to sin, we should accept that sin as bondage. Would anyone voluntarily enter a prison or allow himself or herself to be bound? We become miserable when we are bound by sin. Pray that God will reveal to you anything in your life that is not pleasing to Him, so that you can experience liberty with Him.

2 Corinthians 3:17 says, "Now the Lord is that Spirit; and where the Spirit of the Lord is, there is liberty."

We should be aware that our virtue is assaulted continually by the Devil. He tells us we need power, money, popularity, and good looks, but most of all to be accepted by the world. We are made to feel inadequate or rejected if we don't measure up. Young people are particular targets because of their desire to fit in. Let's examine what God tells us about this topic.

Read 2 Corinthians 3:5. Does anyone (regardless of power, money, or prestige) have any right to think highly of himself or herself? _____

Read 1 Timothy 6:17. What does this say about riches?

_____

Read all of Romans 12. How are our bodies to be presented unto God?

_____

If we want to please God, are we trying to be accepted by the world? (verse two) _____

Are we to be proud or conceited? (verse three)

_____

Do we all have the same gifts? (verse six)

_____

Are to prefer our brother over ourselves? (verse ten)

_____

Are we to be lazy? (verse eleven) _____

How are we to face trials? (verses twelve to fifteen)

_____

How are we to treat people who mistreat us? (verses seventeen to twenty) _____

Read 1 Corinthians 3:21. Are we to glory in any man?

_____

Read 1 Peter 5:6. Are we to exalt ourselves?

_____

Think for a few minutes how contradictory these truths are to what the world entices us to do. Through television, movies, music, magazines, and fashion, the world tells us we are to:

1) Abuse or misuse our bodies;
2) Seek money and power;
3) Seek pleasure through material gain or sinful lusts;
4) Exalt movie stars, musicians, and athletes;
5) Please ourselves (we deserve it);
6) Seek revenge if someone mistreats us;
7) Blame someone else when we fail;
8) Look for release from problems through alcohol, drugs, or other sinful things;
9) Claim "anger" problems if things don't go our way;
10) Reject God because anything spiritual is not "exciting."

You could probably think of more ways our senses (lust of eyes and ears) are assaulted by the Devil. *See* all of these things as tools of Satan and remind yourself every day that he is the author of lies and evil.

When you are tempted, remember these Scriptures:

2 Timothy 2:22: "Flee also youthful lusts: but follow righteousness, faith, charity, peace, with them that call on the Lord out of a pure heart."

James 4:7: "Submit yourselves therefore to God. Resist the devil, and he will flee from you."

Read 1 Corinthians 10:13. Is He able to make a way for you to escape temptation? _____

Rest assured that when you submit to God and resist the Devil, you will find "joy unspeakable and full of glory."

Chapter 6

Virtue: Being Robbed

As we learn more about God's Word, He reveals our weaknesses and sins that we might not have even been aware of (bitterness, envy, malice, hatred, rebellion). If we refuse to know more about God's Word, we are allowing the Devil to rob us of peace and blessings.

God wants us to be clean to the very core of our being. This requires complete submission to Him. Our daily prayer should be that we not become blind to the fact that sin does exist in our lives. Read Matthew 23:25-28. Take heed to the warning Jesus gave to religious people.

You must not be tempted to read God's Word with the thought in mind that someone else needs this. God's Word is personal to each and every individual.

When we see sin in others, we should love them and pray for them. The Lord may give you the opportunity to talk with people about their sins, but it must be done in His Spirit and not because you feel superior to them. It must be done in love and at His time. Look at Proverbs 15:23.

Areas in which we may be unknowingly bound to sin are the following:

Unforgiveness—Reluctance to forgive those who have hurt us. Unless we let God help us, this hurt is like an open wound that will not heal. Recognize your inability to do anything except surrender this hurt to Him; forgive them (even if they don't ask you to) and you can be set free. We cannot ask forgiveness of Him if we haven't forgiven others.

Pride—Read Proverbs 16:5. This means pride in having good looks, money, popularity, brains, or power. It also can mean pride because you feel self-righteousness. James 4:6 says, "Wherefore he saith, God resisteth the proud, but giveth grace unto the humble."

Matthew 23:12: "And whosoever shall exalt himself shall be abased; and he that shall humble himself shall be exalted."

Rebellion—Read Isaiah 1:19-20. What is the promise if we are obedient?

_____

Envy—Read Proverbs 14:30. Envy is a cloak that flatters no one. Often envy and jealousy are an issue of pride because one feels as though one is entitled to what someone else has or that one deserves it more.

Read Proverbs 4:20-27. What parts of our bodies are referred to in this Scripture?

_____

Read Proverbs 28:13-14. What happens when we refuse to confess sin and harden our hearts?

_____

_____

As with faith, virtue is not something we reach perfection with. It needs to be a daily search for truth and application in our lives. Again, God's Word is like a letter to you personally. Know that He loves you unconditionally and His authority is for your good, not harm. Accept His love, strive to love Him more, and obedience becomes a joy rather than a burden.

Chapter 7

KNOWLEDGE

The second attribute to be added to our faith is knowledge. What kind of knowledge is referred to in 2 Peter 5:5?

_____

_____

We need to *know* who God is and all His qualities, including power, greatness, love, mercy, faithfulness, and judgment. Knowledge is not just knowing what the Bible says—true knowledge and discernment of truth comes from first-hand experience. Knowledge is acquired by study, prayer, experience, and practice.

God, through His love and mercy, sent His only begotten Son into this world to live a perfect life and die on the cross for our sins. Our experience of salvation gave us the gift of eternal life. We now have the knowledge of saving grace (not of ourselves, lest any man should boast) (Ephesians 2:8-9).

Read John 15:1-7. Herein is the reason we should gain knowledge of God's Word. If we are not growing, we are withering.

How do we gain spiritual knowledge?

Read Proverbs 1:7. What is the beginning of knowledge?

_____

Read 2 Peter 1:20-21. In order to learn what God wants, we must be teachable students. If we decide we are scholars and we read the Bible with the idea that we are going to prove what we believe, we are deceiving ourselves since we are gaining nothing but pride.

Unless our motivation is pure (we acknowledge that *all our* knowledge is vanity), the Holy Spirit will not help us to discern what God is telling us. Remind yourself of Ephesians 4:17: "Walk not as other Gentiles walk, in the vanity of their mind." Once we know what His Word says, we should obey it.

The vanity of our minds is self-deception. The opposite of knowledge is ignorance. If we are not honest with ourselves, we are without knowledge and become delusional. God's Word teaches us to first be honest with ourselves and fear God, whom no one can deceive.

Read Matthew 6:21. What is your treasure?

_____

_____

Even if you don't write anything at all here, please answer this question to yourself very honestly. God knows what your treasure is! He wants you to acknowledge it for yourself.

As with faith and virtue, knowledge is something we never master. God wants us to read His Word daily, seeking fresh insight. Before you begin to read, pray that God will speak to your heart through His Word. Then be receptive to what He is saying. Remind yourself that these words are addressed to *you,* not someone else!

Read Proverbs 2:2-9. Is there a compelling reason given to study God's Word? _____

Read Proverbs 8:17. Do you love the Lord?

_____

We can never love Him as much as He loves us. Our desire should be to learn to love Him more.

Are there rewards for seeking the Lord? _____

List times in your own life God has answered prayer when you sought him:

_____

_____

_____

_____

Read Proverbs 1:33. What is the promise?

_____

_____

By no means can we grasp all the knowledge we need in a short time. My burden here is to point out some instructions, promises, and warnings from God's Word that are *treasures*. It is my prayer that you will be encouraged and motivated to know more by diligent study for yourself.

Chapter 8

KNOWLEDGE: ACCEPTABLE SERVICE

Read Philippians 4:8. Name some things our thoughts should be on: _____, _____, _____, _____, _____.

Read Galatians 6:10, Romans 12:18-20, and Titus 3:2. Name some ways we should treat others: _____, _____, _____, _____, _____, _____, _____.

Read Matthew 5:44-45. How should we treat our enemies?

_____

Now read Proverbs 16:7. What is the promise given with regard to our enemies?

_____

_____

Read the following Scriptures and note what is acceptable to Christ:

Proverbs 11:28 _____

Proverbs 12:22_____

Proverbs 16:32_____

Proverbs 17:27-28 _____

Proverbs 18:24_____

Proverbs 21:23_____

Proverbs 23:17_____

Matthew 6:14-15 _____

Matthew 6:19-20 _____

Hebrews 12:1-2 _____

Read Matthew 22:37-40. What did Jesus tell us the greatest commandments are?

1) _____

2) _____

Search for knowledge from God's Word! As we apply His Word to our lives, God proves Himself faithful to fulfill His promises. When we reap blessings from obedience, we then gain knowledge of His honesty and faithfulness.

Chapter 9

KNOWLEDGE: WARNINGS AND PROMISES

Read the following Scriptures and name practices we are warned against:

Psalms 37:8 _____

Proverbs 11:2 _____

Proverbs 15:1 _____

Proverbs 16:18 _____

Proverbs 18:9 _____

Proverbs 27:4 _____

Proverbs 31:30 _____

Luke 6:37 _____

There are consequences to following carnal practices. When we experience God's chastening hand on us, we have the knowledge of His judgment. Be thankful that you have experienced His forgiveness and mercy.

Read Hebrews 12:5-6. What quality does God display when He is chastening us? _____ Accept His love!

Read Ephesians 3:13. What does He seek to accomplish through tribulation in our lives?

_____

_____

The following are Scriptures regarding trials and temptations. Make a brief note beside each Scripture about what this means to you:

Psalms 30:5   _____

Psalms 61:2   _____

Proverbs 3:11-12   _____

Isaiah 41:10   _____

Romans 12:14   _____

Philippians 4:7   _____

Hebrews 4:15-16   _____

One of the most powerful verses of Scripture in the Bible is Psalms 46:10: "Be still, and know that I am God . . . ."

There are times when we need to stop our activity (busy lives, trying to figure things out ourselves, our constant making requests of God) and allow Him to speak to us. As my daughter once said to me, "Be quiet long enough to hear Him." Recognize how great He is yet how much He loves you! Recognize He is all powerful and we are all powerless without Him. When you have gone through trials and allowed Him to help you, you gain the knowledge that He is God! He is worthy to be trusted.

Chapter 10

TEMPERANCE

Temperance in a biblical context means "moderation." Moderation means observing reasonable limits. A temperate person displays self-control.

In Galatians 5:22-23, temperance is listed as an attribute of the fruit of the Spirit. Although there are not a lot of Scriptures regarding temperance or moderation, it is obviously a very important attribute of the Christian life.

Philippians 4:5 says, "Let your moderation be known unto all men."

Read Proverbs 25:27-28. If we lack self-control, we are like a city with no defenses. This is an invitation to Satan to assault us.

The opposite of moderation is excess. Lacking temperance would cause us to abuse the good things God has so freely given.

Read 1 Corinthians 9:24-27. These verses speak about running a race. Verse twenty-five says, "Every man that striveth for the mastery is temperate in all things."

Are we in a race? _____ What does it mean to obtain an incorruptible crown?

_____

Without even realizing it, we may have just dropped out of the race. If there is an aspect of your life that causes you problems or causes problems for everyone around you, you may have given in to the lie of the Devil that "God just made you that way and there is nothing you can do about it." Yes, we are flawed humans, but He wants to perfect us. That does not mean we will ever be sinless, but we should be striving for the mastery.

Consider Psalms 139:14. Does this not give us reason to praise him? _____

Does He give everyone gifts? Read 1 Corinthians 7:7. Are all our gifts the same? _____

Now the big question is this: To whose glory do you use the gifts He has given? To answer this question honestly, you must search your heart and ask yourself if the way you spend your day and your life is to please yourself or please Him.

Yes, life is very busy and there are many things that are required of us. Are you spending time doing things that He does not require because it just makes you feel good? It is very easy for us to decide that it is okay to be *excessive* about something so long as we don't see it as sinful or it does not hurt anybody else.

Another thing we should realize is that the Devil will assault us when we are stressed, anxious, or worried. How often do you lose self-control when things are not going so well. I have recently experienced some things that caused me to feel that everything was out of control. I spent several miserable days before I came to the Lord begging for forgiveness and mercy and claimed the power of Jesus over the Devil. Jesus helps us to exercise self-control when we have the courage to look to Him.

Chapter 11

TEMPERANCE:
IS HE YOUR MASTER?

Many times in the Scriptures, Christ was called by the name "Master." Let's examine the definitions of the word *master*. When used as a noun (person), the meaning is "one having authority over another." When used as a verb, the meaning is to "overcome."

If He is not our Master, we will be mastered by sin and our own human nature. When we allow Christ to be our Master, He helps us to not only see our flaws but to overcome them. When, through Him, we make changes, He is glorified.

If we are excessive about anything (even good things), we have allowed ourselves to be mastered by that thing and that is sin. We have to sincerely desire that changes be made. Many times, this is a painful process. We need to pray that He will change the desires of our heart. With His help, we can be victorious over sin.

We deceive ourselves if we refuse to let His Word strip away all the layers of self-righteousness and pride. His healing only comes when we acknowledge our flaws to Him and seek His help.

Look at 1 Corinthians 6:12-20. What is the warning in verse twelve regarding good things?

_____

We should be careful that we are not brought under the power of anything except God.

Look carefully at verses nineteen and twenty of 1 Corinthians 6. How should we view our own bodies?

Read Proverbs 13:3-4. What things are we being told to be temperate in?

_____ , _____

Read Proverbs 23:21. What is the warning here?

_____

_____

What does it mean to be a glutton? _____

What does it mean to be a sluggard? _____

Read Proverbs 25:16-17. Do you often "overdo" something?

_____

Why? _____

Read James 1:19. Name the three things we are told to do:
1) _____ ;
2) _____ ;
3) _____ .

Read Isaiah 58:11: "And the Lord shall guide thee continually, and satisfy thy soul in drought, and make fat thy bones: and thou shalt be like a watered garden, and like a spring of water, whose waters fail not."

Christ alone guides us in straight paths, where we learn temperance.

Chapter 12

PATIENCE

What is patience? The dictionary describes patience as "steadfast despite opposition, difficulty, or adversity." Steadfast brings to mind something that is not easily moved. Does God move?

Ask yourself the question: am I patient? The best way we can clearly see if we can answer yes to this question is to look at the opposite—impatient. How often do we *lose our cool* over situations or people? Reflect on situations—when you are driving, when you are on the phone with customer service of some business, when your order at a restaurant is mixed up. Reflect on how often you display impatience with people around you. It might be a good idea to ask one of your family members (and be willing to accept) how he or she views your level of patience.

We must understand that learning patience is not just a knowledge virtue—it is an experience we go through that forces us to look to Christ and draw strength from Him and accept the lesson he wants us to learn. The difficulty of the experience depends on how long it takes us to get it.

Read Romans 5:2-5. Do we go through tribulations for a reason? God wants us to learn patience or steadfastness. Do we go through this learning process without hope that it will ever end?

Read Hebrews 10:35-37. Where is our hope?

_____

The Scripture that comes to mind over and over again when we think about waiting is Psalms 27:14: "Wait on the Lord: be of good courage, and he shall strengthen thine heart: wait, I say, on the Lord."

Read Isaiah 40:31. What things are we promised if we wait upon the Lord?

_____

_____

Why do we seek patience? Because we are waiting for something to change. The two primary areas in which we desire change are our circumstances and someone whom we are dealing with.

Let's address our desire for change in our circumstances.

Read Philippians 4:11. Do you pray for contentment in your circumstances? _____ Maybe God wants you right where you are.

Read Isaiah 43:2. What does he say we will endure?

_____

_____

Notice the first word of this Scripture is "when" and not "if."

Read 1 Peter 4:12-13. Write in your own words what this means to you:

_____

_____

_____

_____

Recognize that if you are in difficult circumstances, if God brings you to a place, His grace is sufficient to get you through it. Look for the lessons He is trying to teach you through trials.

Is He fair? Read Psalms 18:30.

Is He faithful? Read Psalms 46:1.

Can you trust Him? Read Psalms 18:2.

Circumstances in which we find ourselves can be of our own making or the consequences of sin. If you know what the sin is, God is waiting on you to confess and turn from it. We sometimes feel far from God. We know it is never God's fault. He does not move. We must constantly open our hearts to His convicting power so that He can reveal sin to us.

Can we believe that God can change our circumstances? Certainly He has the power to perform miracles. But often, that is not the way He gets the most glory. More times than not, He gets glory through our being changed or learning to wait on Him.

His desire is to cleanse us completely—that we die to our selfish desires. If your personal desires are more important to you than seeking God's will, you need to recognize this fact. You might think, *I am not living in sin and it feels all right to follow this pattern of behavior.*

Read Proverbs 3:5. Can you trust your mind?_____

Read Jeremiah 17:9. Can you trust your heart?_____

Who is worthy to be trusted? _____

God wants us to seek His will more than seeking to satisfy our personal desires. Matthew 16:25 says, "For whosoever will save his life shall lose it: and whosoever will lose his life for my sake shall find it." Christ wants us to submit ourselves completely to Him for His use.

Sometimes the Lord is waiting for us to have the courage to do something He has lead in. Fear of failure or rejection or feelings of inadequacy can lead us to neglect His work. Psalms 31:24 says, "Be of good courage, and he shall strengthen your heart, all ye that hope in the Lord."

Maybe you reason that your heart is telling you the way things should be. If this is in conflict with God's Word, you need to have a heart change. Are you willing to admit the conflict? Can He change our heart's desire? _____

Pride and selfishness can cause us to be unwilling to surrender to His will. Read Ecclesiastes 7:8-9. Is it evident that the end result is what matters, not the moment?

Sometimes the changes come on God's timetable rather than ours. Read Psalms 40:1-3. What is the promise here? _____

Again, that is for His utmost glory. When we live our lives seeking His glory, He is pleased.

Chapter 13

PATIENCE: PEOPLE IN YOUR LIFE

Do you need patience in dealing with people? The very first question you must ask yourself is this: is this relationship within God's will? If the relationship even hints of being sinful, you need to cut it off. Without any doubt, God is not pleased and will not honor that type of relationship.

We are sometimes forced to have relationships with people who do not have our best interests at heart, either natural or spiritual. This could be people we work with, go to school with, live near, or even go to church with. Through God's Word, you can learn to discern when people you encounter fall into this category. Maybe dealing with a difficult person is your portion of suffering.

How do we deal with these people? We know God wants us to be a light in the world. He wants us, through Him, to influence those we come in contact with, rather than our being influenced by sinful relationships. If a person's actions cause us to react in a negative way, we must acknowledge this before God and seek His help on a daily, if not minute-by-minute, basis. More times than not, the least said, the better the outcome. Proverbs 21:23

states, "Whoso keepeth his mouth and his tongue keepeth his soul from troubles."

Read Psalms 37 and understand the end of evil people. Write some notes here about the comparisons given in these verses between evil and righteousness:

_____

_____

_____

_____

Read Matthew 10:36-40. Why are we surprised when we face opposition from loved ones? Satan knows that those we love can have more power over us. It is possible to put our loved ones ahead of God. When we realize this, we must ask forgiveness and talk to God about our concern for this person rather than trying to *fix* them ourselves. Living before them as a godly example is much more effective than our sermons.

If we find that someone does not want our influence in his or her life, if possible, we need to seek space between us and that person. As my daughter says, "There are some people you have to love from afar." How do you fill the space between yourself and that person? Be careful that your feelings are not pride, self-righteousness, vengeance, bitterness, or resentment. Be sure you are willing to forgive. Do not cease praying for that person. If this is someone close to you, you must daily lay this relationship at God's feet and ask for His guidance in the relationship. Recognize the boundaries of your responsibility to this person.

Recognize that if the person you are seeking patience with is unsaved, you have a great responsibility to seek his or her salvation. In other words, you must not only talk the talk but walk the walk. Most people can discern a shallow person rather quickly (especially if they live with you). If they are saved, however, they may not be seeking spiritual growth as you are. If this is the case, be thankful God is working on *you* and pray for them.

Prayer from a pure heart is powerful. Only God possesses the power to change lives. So in dealing with others, we must do as we are instructed in Proverbs 16:3: "Commit thy works unto the Lord, and thy thoughts shall be established." We also must believe as Paul stated in 2 Timothy 1:12: "For I know whom I have believed, and am persuaded that he is able to keep that which I have committed unto him against that day."

Chapter 14

Patience: Hard Lessons

When I began this study, I really thought I knew about patience. I had two young children! Since that time, there have been trials in my life—some obvious to others, while there has been personal suffering. My son had cancer and went through treatment when he was sixteen years old. Praise God, he was healed. The Lord used many people to support our family through this trial.

Hidden suffering is a totally different problem. One thing I have learned: the hidden suffering should make us less judgmental of others. I do not believe that we are to go about discussing our personal struggles (especially if it leads to embarrassment to anyone). That is not to say that we should not seek counsel or encouragement from fellow believers. This should be done with prayerful consideration.

The way we treat others will affect how God deals with us. As I write these words, I am fearful to ask God to teach me more patience because I am beginning to understand how one gains patience. I can only point you to Christ and His wonderful mercy and grace.

Read James 1:1-8. Can we endure trials with joy?

James 1:3-4. "Knowing this, that the trying of your faith worketh patience. But let patience have her perfect work, that ye may be perfect and entire, wanting nothing."

We need to keep in mind that trials may come for the benefit of others around us. Those around us may be watching while we are in the midst of the fire to see how we will react. When we waver in our faith during trials, the Devil wins the victory. Look again at James 1:6-8. What does this mean to you?

_____

_____

Read 1 Peter 2:20: "For what glory is it, if, when ye be buffeted for your faults, ye shall take it patiently? but if, when ye do well, and suffer for it, ye take it patiently, this is acceptable with God." One of the hardest lessons I have ever had to learn was that I had no right to play the blame game for the trials I faced. Much of my suffering has been because of my sin.

There have been times, however, that I knew my family had been mistreated. I am so thankful that the Lord helped me to understand that when I forgave completely and left the hurt at His feet, I was set free and strengthened to face the trial. His mercy is so complete that when we forgive, we immediately begin to *see the light at the end of the tunnel.* In other words, his blessings become quickly apparent. When I asked for forgiveness, I could forgive myself. I could forgive those who had wronged me or my family. My thoughts toward them could be loving and compassionate. I could pray for them and desire God's mercy for their sin.

Read Psalms 138:8: "The Lord will perfect that which concerneth me: thy mercy, O Lord, endureth for ever: forsake not the works of thine own hands." How sweet is the assurance that, although we walk in the midst of trouble, He is there and will strengthen us. There *is* joy in enduring trials when we know He will never leave us nor forsake us, no matter what we face.

Recall the meaning of patience at the beginning of this study: "Steadfast despite opposition, difficulty or adversity." Steadfast faith in the promises of Christ will see us through adversity.

When we learn the lessons He is seeking to teach in our trials, we gain the experience of patience. Patience is not something we learn unless we experience His mercy and grace. His mercy will flow from us toward others, not just those of our choosing, but everyone. From this study, is it evident that He is patiently waiting for us to see ourselves as He does? Have you seen any area in your life that God is seeking to bring about change?

Consider 1 Peter 5:10. What is He seeking to accomplish through our suffering?

_____

_____

The question here is this: do we want to be made perfect, *stablished*, strengthened, and settled? Or do we want our way and our comfort more? This is indeed a serious question. We should be able to honestly answer yes to the first question before we move on to the next quality we are to add to our faith: godliness.

Chapter 15

GODLINESS

1 Timothy 3:16 says, "And without controversy great is the mystery of godliness . . . ."

The dictionary tells us that godliness means "pious" or "devoted." Pious means "marked by or showing reverence for deity and devotion to divine worship." The Greek root word for godliness is *eusebeia,* meaning "piety" or "spiritual maturity." Frequently, when this word was used in the New Testament world, it described respect for Greek and Roman gods. This may explain why biblical writers more often used the words *faithful* and *righteous* to describe a life pleasing to God.

Consider who your *god* really is! You probably do not worship a pagan god. However, as we have already seen through Scripture, anything we put ahead of God is an idol.

Scriptures pertaining to godliness encourage a pattern or pursuit of behavior acceptable to God. However, godliness is more than correct behavior.

Consider how much the Devil delights in Christians striving to live a clean moral life being deceived into believing that "their"

51

good deeds gave them the right to claim spiritual maturity. These are the very people who do the most damage to the reputation of Christ. They desire the glory for themselves. To truly be godly, when God looks at us He must see Christ. Spiritual maturity causes one to have the heart of a servant for God (not all about being seen or heard, but quietly busy with the work God gives them to do).

Read Galatians 2:20. What does this say to you about living acceptably?

_____

_____

We have to let go of our selfish natures and desires in order that Christ, through the Holy Spirit, reigns in us. Our attitude must be surrender of *all* of ourselves to His will. We must see Him as He is and see ourselves as completely powerless without Him.

So our godliness is not measured with how *perfect* we consider our lives or the outward appearances. Rather, our godliness is measured by how humbly and meekly we are submitting ourselves to Him. How much are you dying to self? How often do you feel that you have rights?

_____

What *rights* does a servant have? _____
A word of caution is that we must make sure who we are serving. We must be a servant of God first and foremost.

Read Matthew 11:28-30. Here is the invitation to come to Him and accept His rest.

Now let's consider verse twenty-nine: "Take my yoke upon you and learn of me, for I am meek and lowly in heart; and ye shall find rest unto your souls." Notice He said "my." We all wear some kind of yoke. What is your understanding of what it means to wear a yoke?

_____

To understand whose yoke you are wearing, try asking yourself these questions: Who are you trying to please? Whom do you seek approval or acceptance from? We must use caution not to let anyone come before God in our devotion. Can we take Christ's yoke upon us if we are serving another god? _____ Read Matthew 6:24.

Can you be your own god? _____ If we put our desires or wishes ahead of His will, the answer is yes. If we put others ahead of Him, they become a god to us.

The yoke of sin is a heavy burden. There is nothing about Christ's yoke to hurt us; to the contrary, there is much to refresh us. His yoke is lined with tenderness and love. He said in Matthew 11:30: "For my yoke is easy, and my burden is light."

Read 2 Timothy 3:12. What is the burden a godly person bears? _____ Our willingness to suffer comes from love and thanksgiving to Christ for the gift of salvation. Are we willing?

Now go back to Matthew 11:29: "For I am meek and lowly in heart . . . ." How often do we compare ourselves to others in order to feel good about ourselves? Read 2 Corinthians 10:12-18. Are we warned about the deceit of comparing ourselves to others? _____ We must seek the heart of Jesus for our godliness to be anything other than a mockery. The godly person is not about proving how right he is but rather knows his need to be made right.

Read all of Romans 12. This is a wonderful and practical chapter for a person striving for godliness. Write your own notes about things we are told to do in this chapter.

_____

_____

_____

_____

_____

_____

_____

_____

Chapter 16

GODLINESS: THE POWER

Look at 2 Timothy 3:5. It is possible to possess a "form of godliness" while denying its power. Read 2 Peter 1:3. (The basis for this study begins at verse five).

What is the power that we can deny? _____ Christ, by his life, death, and resurrection, created our access to God. We, of ourselves, have nothing to offer God. Look at Isaiah 64:6. What does this verse say to you?

_____

Read Galatians 3:3. We have already learned that only through Christ do we have the ability to walk godly. He left His Spirit to live within us and grant us the power to please Him. What a wonderful gift!

How is a godly person recognized? Appearances can be deceptive! Read Psalms 63:5. What do people whose souls are satisfied speak of? _____ Do they talk about what *they* have done? _____ Or do they talk about what Christ has done for them? _____

Let's closely examine Galatians 5. In verse one, notice that Paul was teaching the Galatians to "Stand fast therefore in the liberty wherewith Christ hath made us free, and be not entangled again with the yoke of bondage." The Galatians were holding on to the law for justification (that Christ's death was not sufficient for salvation). Paul taught them that their beliefs were a yoke of bondage to them. Recall how you felt just after you were saved. Did you feel free? _____

Again, remember 2 Corinthians 3:17: "Now the Lord is that Spirit: and where the Spirit of the Lord is, there is liberty."

What happens that causes us to feel heavy burdened? Are you in bondage to sin or self-imposed expectations? _____ Are you in prison to someone else laying their guilt at your feet? _____ Is your focus on your performance? _____

After reading Galatians 5:14-15, relate how the law is fulfilled.

_____

_____

You can know a tree by the fruit it bears. Read Galatians 5:22-23 and list the fruit of the Spirit: _____, _____, _____, _____, _____, _____, _____, and _____. What does everyone else see in you? We deceive ourselves if we do not allow God to reveal to us what kind of fruit we are bearing.

Galatians 5:26: Are we warned about seeking glory?

_____

Read 1 Timothy 6:6: What is great gain?

_____

From personal experience, resentment and bitterness are the result of attempting to serve God with what *feels* right. Remember that our minds and even our hearts are deceitful. Only through the power of the Holy Spirit can our devotion and worship be acceptable. We must die to self! He alone is worthy of glory!

Chapter 17

BROTHERLY KINDNESS

What is brotherly kindness? The Scripture in 2 Peter 1 that is the focus of this study is the only biblical reference to the exact term "brotherly kindness." However, there are many biblical references to "kindness" and particularly "lovingkindness" when referring to God's treatment of His own.

Think for a few minutes of the opposite of kindness. I will list a few words that reflect the opposite of kindness: meanness, nastiness, malice, viciousness, ruthlessness, and harshness. We need to sincerely ask the Lord to reveal if we are *ever* guilty of treating *anyone* in this manner. More importantly, do we have any of these thoughts toward others? Do any of these traits speak of love or genuine concern?

Kindness is an act motivated by love. Some of the synonyms of kindness are as follows: compassion, sympathy, gentleness, and thoughtfulness. Brotherly kindness is a quality that speaks of action. The second greatest commandment given by Jesus's own words in Matthew 22:39 is "Thou shalt love thy neighbor as thyself."

Read the following verses and note the specific instruction given to us regarding love and the action it should prompt:

Proverbs 3:27-30

_____

_____

_____

_____

1 John 3:17

_____

_____

_____

_____

John 13:34-35

_____

_____

_____

_____

Romans 12:10

_____

_____

_____

_____

Ephesians 4:32

_____

_____

_____

_____

Colossians 3:12-17

_____

_____

_____

_____

1 Thessalonians 4:8-9

_____

_____

_____

_____

The above Scriptures instruct that loving each other and being kind are not optional but commands from God if we are to please Him. At first glance, adding brotherly kindness does not seem like a hard thing to do. It is very easy to be kind to those who are kind and loving toward you.

Be honest, how do you respond to those who are less than kind to you? *Honesty with yourself and to God is essential for spiritual growth.* God knows the truth and He knows when you are deceiving yourself.

Read Luke 6:27-38. Write what this Scripture says to you:

_____

_____

_____

_____

These are Jesus's own words. This completely takes away our right to decide who we can show mercy and kindness to. Society and our own self-righteousness mold us into a prideful position of prejudice against anyone who does not think like we do. This does not mean that we are not to recognize and hate sin. But we are to love the sinner.

Chapter 18

BROTHERLY KINDNESS: OUR MOTIVATION

We must acknowledge that we do not like to show acts of kindness to those who are unlovable. But the commandment is that we love our neighbors as ourselves, not just those we like and who are grateful! It is our duty to love the unlovable and to be kind to everyone.

In order for us to truly recognize where we stand with regard to our acts of kindness, we have to question what our motivation is.

1) Is our focus on how it will make us feel to do something good for someone?

2) What are we going to get out of this?

3) Would you perform this act of kindness if no one knew you were doing it?

4) If the recipient of the act did not know where it came from, would you still do it?

5) Do you consider how much time and money an act of kindness will cost you?

6) Is your motivation for favor or glory?

God does not expect our acts of kindness to be beyond our physical or financial means. Therefore, not only our motivations but the timing should be prayerfully considered. Sometimes a kind word is all that He asks of us. Let Him direct you when and how to reach out to someone. Open your heart to opportunities to help others.

The only motivation that is pure and acceptable is the one motivated by our desire to follow His command and reveal Christ to others, regardless of how it is accepted or the cost, in time, effort, or money.

We have to be willing to be kind even when we know the act may not be appreciated or we may not receive even a thank-you. When God puts it on your heart, you can know He sees your willingness and your effort will not go unnoticed.

Read 1 Thessalonians 3:12-13: "And the Lord make you to increase and abound in love one toward another, and toward all men, even as we do toward you: To the end he may stablish your hearts unblameable in holiness before God, even our Father, at the coming of our Lord Jesus Christ with all his saints."

There is clear motivation in this verse—to be "unblameable in holiness before God" is something worth striving for.

Read John 15:12-18. Write in your own words what this Scripture means to you:

_____

_____

_____

_____

Our motivation to serve must come with the knowledge that we will suffer and, just as Jesus was misunderstood and mistreated, so we will be.

Chapter 19

BROTHERLY KINDNESS: THE "HOW-TO"

When we open our hearts to the truth of God's Word, we see that Jesus's commandments are not something we ourselves possess the ability to do. We just do not have it in us to love everyone. God does not give us an instruction without providing what we need to follow through.

Read John 15:1-11. Herein lies the *how to* for following Jesus's commandment—abiding in Christ. Only when we submit every part of our hearts to Him and humble ourselves before Him can we see that Calvary meant the same thing for all men as it did for us. Without Him, we are nothing. Only through His love in us can we love the unlovable. His love should flow freely through us to others. We are merely a vessel for His use.

Read Galatians 6:7-10. Write in your own words what this Scripture says to you:

_____

_____

_____

_____

This is a promise and a warning at the same time. If we sow seeds of kindness, we will reap kindness. Verse nine tells us that we may have to practice some patience. Again, true honesty is necessary for us to know what kind of seeds we are sowing. Recall the first part of verse seven: "Be not deceived; God is not mocked."

Read John 17:21: "That they all may be one; as thou, Father, art in me, and I in thee; that they also may be one in us; that the world may believe that thou hast sent me." Our purpose is to reveal Christ to a lost and dying world. If the members of our church were as one, would not our message be more powerful and our light shine brighter? Our job is not to point fingers or condemn anyone but to intercede on their behalf by prayer.

The deeper meaning in this lesson strips away our pride and all our rights to decide who deserves our love and our kind, generous deeds. We must quit trying to be a god with a little *g*, deciding who is within our realm of affection.

This lesson surely knocks us off the pedestal of self-righteousness and is humbling but nonetheless necessary if we are to grow. We must show mercy, just as He has shown us mercy.

Reread John 15:10-11. Oh, that His joy would be full in me. Only through obedience can we be a vessel of honor unto the Lord.

Chapter 20

CHARITY

It is important to distinguish the meaning of charity from a biblical standpoint as opposed to the secular use. Charity is spoken of in modern-day terms as giving to needy causes or individuals prompted by love or compassion. The dictionary says charity is goodwill toward or love of humanity. We will later fully examine 1 Corinthians 13. For the purposes of clarifying secular referrals to charity, read verse three: "And though I bestow all my goods to feed the poor, and though I give my body to be burned, and have not charity, it profiteth me nothing." Obviously there is much more to charity than giving to needy causes.

The word *charity* is found only in the New Testament and is translated from the Greek word *agape,* meaning "love." Clearly there is a difference in *love* and *charity* in the Bible. Many references to love in the Bible have negative connotations, such as in 1 Timothy 6:10: "For the love of money is the root of all evil." We can love ourselves or things so much that it becomes sinful.

In the biblical sense, charity is God's pure love toward man. This kind of love is not natural for mankind—it is an expression of Christ living within us. This kind of love is directed outward and is completely unselfish. All biblical references to charity refer to a positive quality we are urged to participate in. We can only participate in Christ's pure love through setting aside our own desires and defective thought processes and allowing Him to fill us with His love. Charity is action motivated by God's love.

Read 1 John 4:7-21. The author of 1 John obviously makes clear our obligation to love God and others. These Scriptures leave no room for argument. We must truly love God in order to love others. All mankind was created in love by God. He has given the command that we are to love one another (verse twenty-one).

We can hate the sin of men but we are to love their souls. The reason this is so hard for us is because we are molded and shaped by worldly thought processes inspired by the Devil. We judge who is worthy of our love—what a ridiculous thought. We are all sinners and have no reason for glory. However, if Satan can use saved people to hinder sinners or be at enmity with each other, what a victory for Satan.

To refuse to love and act upon such love is a reflection of multiple sinful characteristics: pride, selfishness, envy, unforgiveness, and being judgmental.

A pure heart is just that—pure—free from worldly defilement. Ego in the sight of God is shameful. We are truly deceived if we are unwilling to let God's love so fill our heart there is no room for any of the above characteristics. If we love Him as we are instructed and allow Him to cleanse our hearts and minds, we can become a reservoir of love that spills over into the lives of others. If we refuse to let go of our twisted egos, we are but slaves to ourselves. John 8:36: "If the Son therefore shall make you free, ye shall be free indeed."

Chapter 21

CHARITY: THE QUALITIES AND EFFECTS

Read the following Scriptures and note what is said regarding charity in each verse:

1 Corinthians 8:1-3 _____

_____

Colossians 3:12-15 _____

_____

1 Peter 4:8 _____

1 Corinthians 13 tells us much about charity. Read this chapter carefully and consider some of the following qualities regarding charity and its effects:

1. Even if we had spiritual gifts of prophecy or speaking in tongues, without charity it would be nothing.

2. Even if we have great knowledge or have faith to move mountains, without charity it is nothing.

3. Charity is long suffering. It can endure mistreatment and misunderstanding without feeling resentment. Charity will put up with mistreatment and patiently wait for the effects love and kindness will have.

4. Charity is kind. We never find an example of Jesus being unkind.

5. Charity envieth not. Envy is the effect of ill will. A heart that loves as Jesus did could not rejoice in bad things happening to others.

6. Charity is not filled with self-importance and is not easily provoked. What makes us feel important? How easily do you get your feelings hurt?

7. Charity is an enemy to selfishness. A heart with love flowing out will never seek its own to the hurt of others.

8. Charity beareth all things; it endureth all things. If we think we are having a lot to bear, all we have to do is think of Calvary and we are reminded of what He did for us and what we face seems trivial. Psalms 34:19: "Many are the afflictions of the righteous: but the Lord delivereth him out of them all."

There are other qualities and effects of charity you may want to list below from the Scriptures we have read.

1. _____

_____

2. _____

_____

3. _____

_____

Read 1 Timothy 4:12 and 2 Timothy 2:22. Note whom these verses are directed to _____. It is possible for everyone who knows Christ to live a righteous life. How? Seek Him with a pure heart.

True charity in our hearts will make us stand out from the crowd. People will see Christ in us. It will be apparent that our strength comes from Him. This may take time. But ultimately the victory can be ours if we do all for His glory.

1 Corinthians 13:12-13: "For now we see through a glass, darkly; but then face to face: now I know in part; but then shall I know even as also I am known. And now abideth faith, hope, charity, these three; but the greatest of these is charity."

These verses speak of the time when we will see Jesus face to face. By faith we can see who He is and know His intentions for us while we live on earth. But our vision is marred by sin that surrounds us. But face to face with Jesus, we will see Him clearly and our faith and hope will become sight. Our faith and hope will be fulfilled, and in His presence our charity will be perfected and know no bounds. Oh, glorious day.

Chapter 22

LOOKING BACK

We will reread 2 Peter 1:1-12. We will look at verse nine carefully. We see the warning that, if a person lacks the graces we are studying, he "is blind and cannot see afar off, and hath forgotten that he was purged from his old sins."

A person in this condition is blind and cannot see forward or back. We will only be able to see our current circumstances: living in a sin-cursed world full of lusts. What is the importance of looking back?

Can Satan make us forget what Christ did for us on Calvary?

_____

Can Satan make us forget God's faithfulness to us?

_____

Can Satan magnify our trials and make us forget God's blessings? _____

Can we look back in our lives, see our mistakes, and learn not to repeat them? _____

When God chastens us, can we look back and acknowledge our sins and ask for mercy? _____

We should not dwell in the past to the extent that we do not accept His forgiveness. However, looking back more clearly helps us to see His hand in our lives. We can reflect on the times we trusted Him and He proved His faithfulness. We can also reflect on the times we rejected Him and had to suffer.

Not only are we encouraged to know Him better, but we have the responsibility to share Him with a lost world by testifying to what He has done for us.

Chapter 23

CONCLUSION

Our spiritual journey should focus completely on Jesus; His life, death, and resurrection. Our value to Him is not measured by our knowledge or deeds. God seeks a heart that acknowledges no right to assert itself. He desires our love and freely gives His love and forgiveness.

Read Isaiah 61:1-3:

The spirit of the Lord God is upon me; because the Lord hath anointed me to preach good tidings unto the meek; he hath sent me to bind up the broken-hearted, to proclaim liberty to the captives, and the opening of the prison to them that are bound;

To proclaim the acceptable year of the Lord, and the day of vengeance of our God; to comfort all that mourn;

To appoint unto them that mourn in Zion, to give unto them beauty for ashes, the oil of joy for mourning, the garment of praise for the spirit of heaviness; that they might be called trees of righteousness, the planting of the Lord, that he might be glorified.

Jesus Himself read from the Book of Isaiah in Luke 4:17-21 regarding His purpose in coming to this earth. Reread these words and *believe* they are meant for you and whatever circumstance you face.

Jesus died on Calvary to save our souls and rose again so that in Him we could have all we need to live peaceful, joyful lives for Him.

Colossians 1:17: "And he is before all things, and by him all things consist."

Philippians 4:19: "But my God shall supply all your need according to his riches in glory by Christ Jesus."

He came to free us and grant us an abundant life—not because of our worth but because of His loving kindness. Find freedom in accepting the boundary of responsibility He gives you—your own heart and mind.

Philippians 1:6: "Being confident of this very thing, that he which hath begun a good work in you will perform it until the day of Jesus Christ."

As we seek Him with a pure heart, we see Him more clearly. He desires close communion with us. He loves us and wants to supply our needs.

His word convicts cleanly and with love. Daily we can be cleansed, refreshed, and renewed. Then our lives can shine the brightest in a dark world.

Never will a spiritually mature person tell you how spiritual he is. 1 Corinthians 1:29: "That no flesh should glory in His presence." The spiritual person will tell you about the One who gave life. The spiritual person will display the fruit of the Spirit. The surrendered heart and mind will spill over with His love and kindness and forgiveness. The spiritual person will lift up Christ, not self. John 12:32: "And I, if I be lifted up from the earth, will draw all men unto me."

About the Author

Abundant blessings in the midst of traumatic events in her life call the author to testify about a life committed to Jesus. Patricia grew up in a small town as the daughter of a Baptist minister. She is a long-time member of her church, where she is the choir pianist.

Patricia lives in Hattiesburg, Mississippi, with her husband Mark and two children: Ned, nineteen, and Grace, seventeen. Patricia is a trained legal secretary but became a stay-at-home mom when Ned was born. In 2010, Patricia went to work with her husband, Mark, who has been practicing law for almost thirty years.

Patricia and her family love to travel and have enjoyed many family trips together. The front cover photo was made by Mark just off the coast of Vancouver Island during a 2010 fishing trip that was disrupted (delightfully so) by a pod of whales. Patricia loves to read, cook, and garden.